D0745022

ENJOY YOUR RECORDER

A New, Complete Method of Instruction for the Recorder, Including Exercises, Reviews, Trill Charts, Ornaments and Embellishments, Duets, Trios, and Quartets

by

The TRAPP FAMILY SINGERS

* * *

"Come, some music!
Come, the Recorder . . ."
W. Shakespeare: Hamlet

Book M-1 for C-Soprano or C-Tenor.
Book M-2 for F-Alto, F-Sopranino, or F-Bass.

MAGNAMUSIC DISTRIBUTORS, Inc.

SHARON, CONN.

ISBN 0-913334-01-4

INTRODUCTION

For ten summers, a large and widely varied group of people from seven to seventy years of age have come to the Trapp Family Music Camp in Stowe, Vermont, for the purpose of learning to play the recorder.

The Trapp Family Singers themselves have played recorders — all of them from the little Sopranino to the imposing Bass — in hundreds of concerts for nearly two decades, in most European countries, in the United States and Canada, in Central and South America, in the Caribbean and in the Hawaiian Islands.

Many of their enthusiastic listeners have turned into eager students and advocates of this ancient and lovely instrument, with its "sweet music" of which the poets sang.

Today, the recorder is again being played as it was centuries ago, and the number of its lovers is increasing day by day. Through the doors which it has opened, many have found great enjoyment in exploring the wealth of lovely music written for it through the ages.

This Method has grown as a consequence of the recorder classes conducted by Maria Trapp in Stowe, Vermont. Ten years of practical experience in the art of teaching the recorder are resolved and set forth in this Method.

It is a distinct pleasure to present this excellent work to the many thousands of lovers of the recorder, and to the many more thousands who will want to join their ranks.

Theodore Mix, President
Magnamusic Distributors, Inc.

December 1, 1953

DEDICATION

We dedicate this Method to each person who discovers the recorder. He will need no further dedication, for the enjoyment of playing together with others, the delightful hours, and the rewarding excursions through recorder literature, will dedicate him more thoroughly than we could ever do in these words or in this Method.

Stowe, Vermont
November 30, 1953

The Trapp Family

ACKNOWLEDGMENT

I would like to express my appreciation for the help and encouragement given to me in the writing of this method. In my own Family, Father Franz Wasner and my brother Werner Trapp wrote most of the two-part settings, and all of the Family helped greatly as they always do. In addition, many others were of great assistance, of whom I would like to mention Mrs. Allston Dana, Mr. and Mrs. Harold Peterson, Professor Maximilian Albrecht, our excellent engraver Mr. Alvin Ranc, Mr. Andrew Gergely for his photographs, and last but not least, Mr. Theodore Mix, president of Magnamusic Distributors, Inc. Their contributions, suggestions, and work were an inspiration most gratefully received.

Maria Trapp

ENJOY YOUR RECORDER

We have not the slightest doubt that you will enjoy your recorder. It will become a companion to you, a means of expression that will give you much satisfaction, and it will prove a bridge of common interest between you and many others as you meet them and explore music together.

We earnestly entreat you to seek others now, as a beginner. Learn with them. Play together and help each other when one has difficulty in some note or passage. Learning by one's self is easy and pleasurable — but learning with others can be twice as enjoyable.

For this reason, we have included many duets in the Lessons. Even if you study alone, practise and master both parts. This will help you when you play with others later. In the Soprano Method, most second Soprano parts are within the range of an Alto Recorder. In the Alto Method, most second Alto parts are within the range of a Tenor recorder. Thus, your choice of friends and other instruments is widened while learning.

HOW TO BUY A RECORDER:

The recorder is a musical instrument and not a toy.

Take your time and choose the best. The recorder must be in tune, pleasing to your ear, with both high and low notes responding easily, and the tone clear. Some prefer a sharper, some a softer tone. The extra time spent in choosing a really good recorder will repay you in the end.

What is the difference between the Baroque and the German Fingering systems?

The main difference lies in the fingering of B♭ and B . (See page 5).

Baroque fingering is the authentic fingering of recorders before, during and since the Baroque period in history, and, until the early 1900's, the only fingering. It has the advantage of an easier B in both the high and low octaves, which makes faster and more accurate passages possible when they involve this note.

German fingering was the result, in about 1920, of a desire to simplify the forked Baroque fingering of B♭ in both the high and low octaves, and a desire to have recorder fingering conform to the Boehm system in clarinets. Its advantages are an easier whole-tone scale, and related fingering to orchestral woodwinds, when used as a pre-orchestral instrument for children.

REGULAR AND ALTERNATE FINGERINGS

There is a fingering for each note which gives the best pitch and is most often used in playing the recorder. We call this the "regular" fingering, and learn it first.

A few notes have "alternate" fingerings, which are also listed. These are of three types, and are explained in each case where they appear.

(1) An "alternate" fingering is one which produces the same note as the "regular" fingering, but may be easier to use when the previous or the following note is very dissimilar to the "regular" fingering of this note. Thus, in going up the scale through a certain note, the "regular" fingering may prove the easiest. Coming down, the "alternate" may be the easiest. Each case is explained in the text.

(2) Another type of "alternate" fingering is given, in a very few cases, because of the difference in makes of recorders. For instance, an "alternate" fingering is given in Lesson VI with the caution to use it only if your particular recorder does not sound true using the "regular" fingering.

(3) Trill fingerings (complete chart of these may be found directly after the "Exercises") are in some cases "alternate" fingerings, too, but only because in playing a trill absolute accuracy of pitch is not as necessary as ease and speed.

HOW TO CARE FOR YOUR RECORDER

A new recorder should be oiled before using it the first time. Take the instrument apart at the joints and oil the inside of each part with a swab dipped sparingly in woodwind oil. Be careful not to oil the aperture (or opening) nor the fipple (plug). (See "Parts of the Recorder" on inside back cover). Let the oil dry twelve hours, then rub off the surplus oil and your new instrument is ready to be played. Occasional oiling (three or four times a year) is good for the preservation of the instrument. Do not oil after playing until it is completely dry.

Never leave the recorder near heat, radiators, nor in the sunlight.

Before Playing: Warm your instrument.

Your recorder must be warm when you start playing to protect the wood against cracking. It also helps to keep moisture from forming in the mouthpiece which blurs the tone. Hold it with your hands until it is thoroughly warm.

During Playing:

Blow gently. Overblowing eventually will ruin the instrument in the higher range.

A new recorder should be broken in slowly, and not played for more than half an hour a day for the first two or three days.

The upper notes require even more gradual breaking in. Spend a few practise sessions on each upper note, starting with the "D".

In the narrow opening between fipple and mouthpiece, moisture sometimes collects and blurs the tone. In this case place the soft part of your fingertip over the aperture and blow sharply.

After Playing: Dry your instrument.

Take your recorder apart and wipe out the inside of each section gently with a dry swab, again being careful not to touch the fipple nor aperture of the mouthpiece. Let it dry completely before storing it in its case or box.

HOW TO HOLD YOUR RECORDER

With The Fingers:

LEFT thumb covers the hole in the back (octave hole)
1st (index) finger covers 1st hole in the front
2nd (middle) finger covers 2nd hole in the front
3rd (ring) finger covers 3rd hole in the front

RIGHT 1st finger covers 4th hole in the front
2nd finger covers 5th hole in the front
3rd finger covers 6th hole in the front
4th finger covers 7th hole in the front

Use the pads of the fingers, and not the tips, to cover the holes.

With The Arms:

Be relaxed and natural.

Hold your arms at a comfortable angle away from your body so that the recorder is held as in the picture. Practise this in front of a mirror.

When fingers of the right hand are not in use for playing, place the third finger between the fifth and sixth hole, with the thumb on the back of the instrument between the fourth and fifth hole, which helps to balance the recorder.

Each finger should play only the holes indicated for it, as listed above.

The Lips:

Hold the mouthpiece between your lips in front of the teeth. Close your lips around the top of the mouthpiece in a relaxed and comfortable position, opening them only to breathe at the end of a phrase or at the breathing marks indicated by a comma above the staff.

HOW TO PLAY THE RECORDER

How To Blow:

There are three stages in producing a tone:

1. The Attack or start.
   To start a note you use your tongue saying "du". This attack is necessary to give the tone a clear and distinct start. This is called tonguing. Every tone is tongued unless it is connected to the preceding note by a slur.
2. Blowing.
   Blow gently and support your breath as you do in singing. Sustain the same pressure throughout to keep your pitch.
   The more pressure, the higher or sharper the pitch.
   The less pressure, the lower of flatter the pitch.
   Even, steady blowing will make your recorder a singing instrument.
3. Closings.
   To end or close your note, bring your tongue against your teeth for a "D" which remains unpronounced. It will be indicated in the lessons like this: D̸

Finger Action:

The three rules of action for the fingers are:

1. Come down like a hammer.
2. Hold tight for the length of the note.
3. Release quickly.

Each finger should play only the holes indicated for it, and when a finger is not in use, it should be held directly above the hole.

To play the recorder well you need coordination of the tongue and fingers, accurate fingering, good breath control, and a singing heart.

What is the difference between the Baroque and the German Fingering systems?

The main difference lies in the fingering of B and B♭.

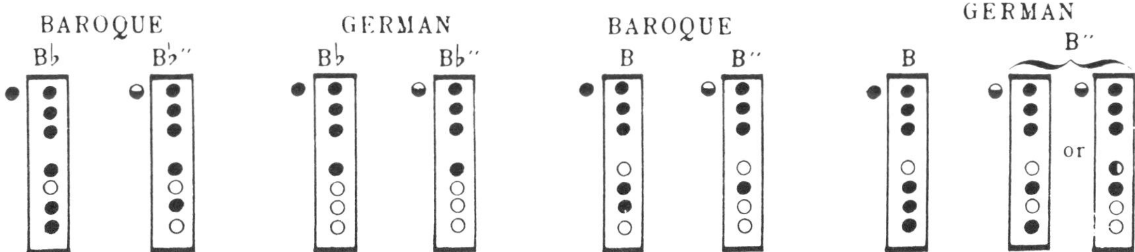

Note: The symbol('') means one octave higher.

SYMBOLS USED IN MUSIC NOTATION

The following is not intended as a substitute for a teacher, for it is neither complete nor self-explanatory. It is to be used as a reference page to help you remember some of the symbols we use in writing music.

The Shape of Notes and Rests

The relative duration (length of time) of a note or rest is indicated by its shape. Although you cannot tell the actual duration of a note by its shape alone, you can tell how it compares with the other notes in the same composition. The following chart will show these relationships:

Each note is twice as long as the note beneath it.

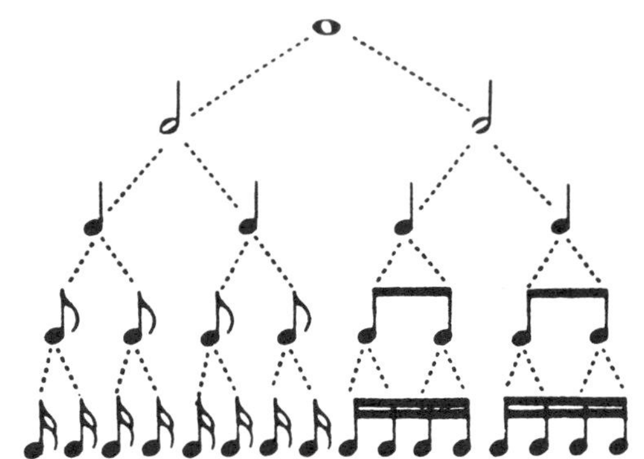

A whole note equals

two half notes, or

four quarter notes, or

eight eighth notes, or

sixteen sixteenth notes.

The same relationships exist among the corresponding rests:

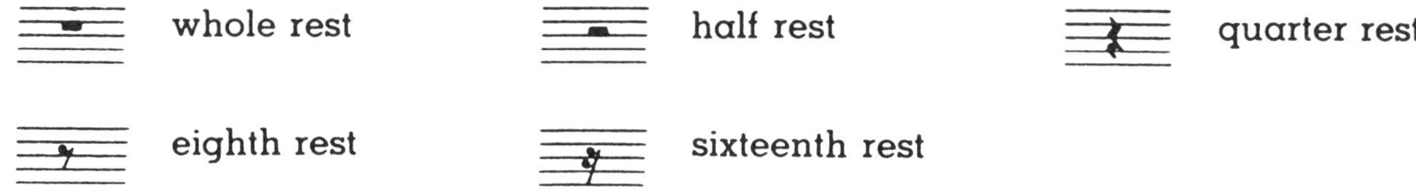

A dot placed beside a note *adds one-half* of the original duration of the note.

Examples: 

The Position Of The Notes On The Staff

The pitch which is represented by a note is indicated by the note's position on the staff. The higher the position on the staff, the higher the pitch to be played. The clef sign placed at the beginning of the staff helps tell the names of the lines and spaces. The "G" or "treble" clef sign marks the line "g" —

The "F" or "bass" clef sign marks the line "f"

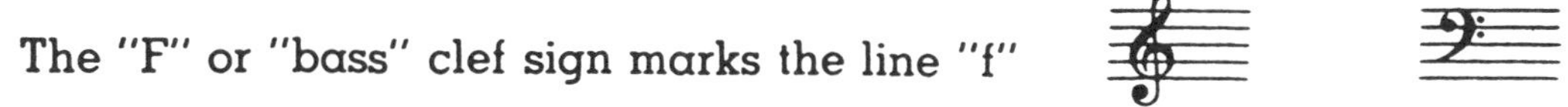

Sometimes it is necessary to cause a line or space to represent a pitch one half-step higher than it normally does. This is indicated by placing a sharp (♯) on the proper line, or in the proper space. Similarly, a line or space can represent a pitch one half-step *lower* by placing a flat (♭) on, or in, it.

Examples: 

When a note or a line has been sharp or flat, it is returned to the natural note by placing the natural (♮) symbol in front of the note or line. This erases the effect of the sharp or flat.

Time Signature

At the beginning of each piece of music, you will find two numbers. These help us to know how the rhythm is to be played. The upper number indicates the number of *beats* in one measure. The lower number indicates the *kind of note* which receives *one beat.*

Examples:		
	$\frac{4}{4}$ or C	— *4* beats in one measure — a *quarter* note receives *one* beat
	$\frac{3}{4}$	— *3* beats in one measure — a *quarter* note receives *one* beat
	$\frac{2}{2}$ or ¢	— *2* beats in one measure — a *half* note receives *one* beat
	$\frac{6}{8}$	— *6* beats in one measure — an *eighth* note receives *one* beat

Miscellaneous Symbols

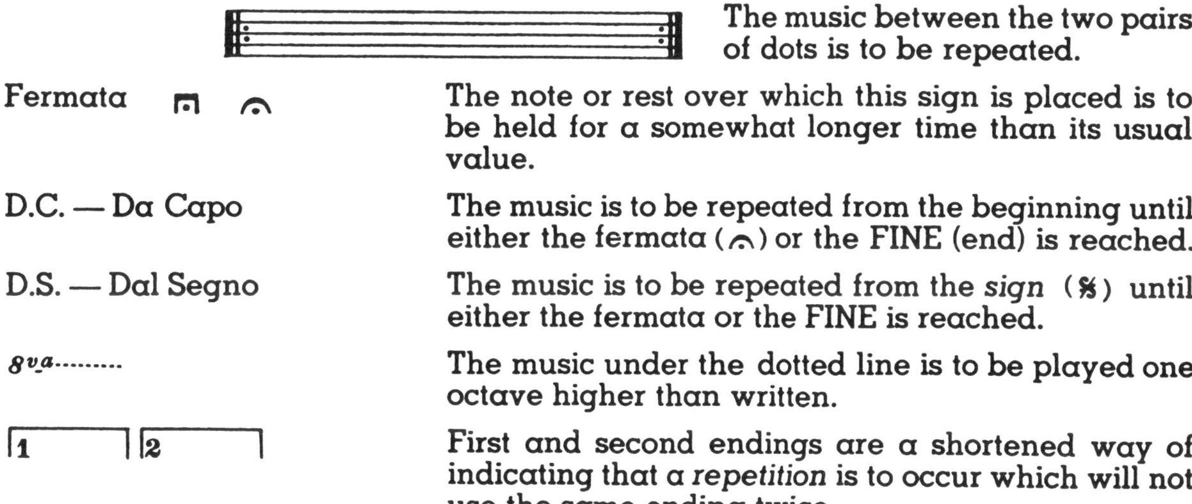

The music between the two pairs of dots is to be repeated.

Fermata — The note or rest over which this sign is placed is to be held for a somewhat longer time than its usual value.

D.C. — Da Capo — The music is to be repeated from the beginning until either the fermata (𝄐) or the FINE (end) is reached.

D.S. — Dal Segno — The music is to be repeated from the *sign* (𝄋) until either the fermata or the FINE is reached.

8va........ — The music under the dotted line is to be played one octave higher than written.

1 | 2 — First and second endings are a shortened way of indicating that a *repetition* is to occur which will not use the same ending twice.

Example:

Written:

Played:

Copyright, 1954 by
The Trapp Family Singers
and
Magnamusic Distributors, Inc.

LESSON 1

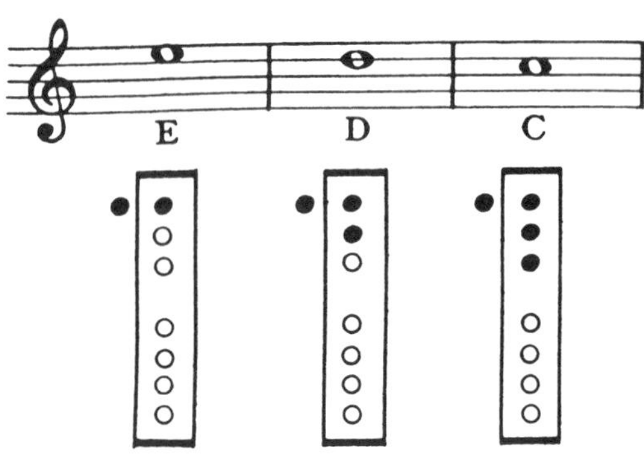

The first lesson is most important. Here you will put into practice what you have learned in the instructions given on pages 4 and 5, the fundamentals of recorder playing. Spend enough time and attention to master them thoroughly.

The first notes you learn are E, D, and C. To finger them you need only the left hand. The right hand supports the instrument as shown in the picture on page 4.

First, try the fingering of E, D, and C without blowing. The fingers should find their holes *by feeling.* Let them act as hammers.

Practise blowing and tonguing just one note (D). Start the note with "Du".

Breathe only at breath-marks (').

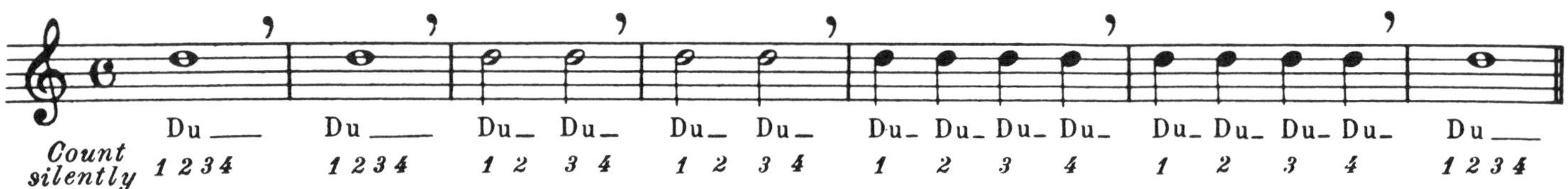

The dash after the "Du" —— is the breath-line. It should remind you to continue blowing until a new note starts, or the note is closed with a "Đ".

Close the notes with "Đ" as explained on page 5.

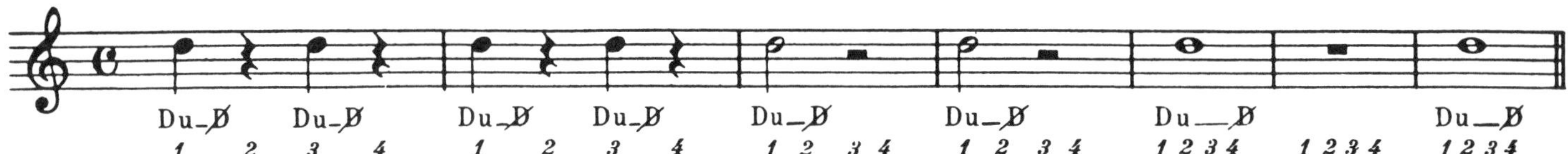

Fingers come down like hammers! Release fingers quickly!

Did you keep blowing the entire length of the notes?

Did you close the notes?

Where is your right hand? Does it support the recorder?

FIRST DUET WITH TEACHER

Did you keep your lips closed around the mouthpiece and use your tongue to start each new note?

Take turns playing these parts:

PUPILS' DUET

How was the position of your fingers?

Did you cover the holes with the soft part of your finger?

MELODY FROM THE NINTH CENTURY

If you know your tonguing and fingering well, you are ready for Lesson II.

Remember to dry your instrument before you put it away!

LESSON II

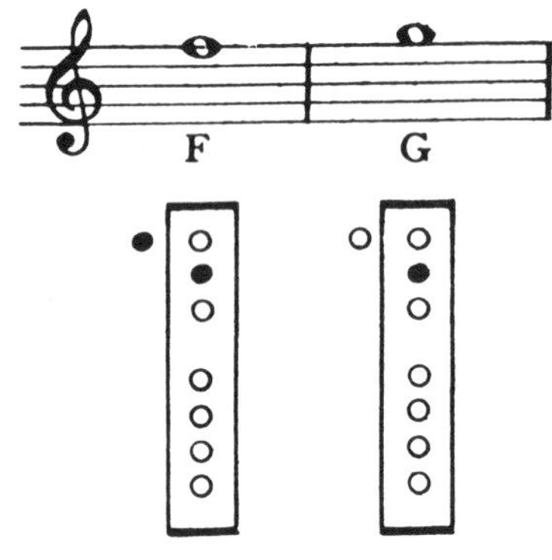

To play G, lift your thumb a short distance from the hole so that it is ready when you need to cover the hole again. Remember that your thumb must act like a hammer, too, and hit and release quickly. In playing G, you have no left thumb to hold the recorder. Your mouth, and the thumb and third finger of your right hand, will support and balance it.

Does your thumb hit the hole right away?

THE SLUR

The slur is a tie which connects two or a group of notes. It is played by tonguing (Du) only the first note of the slur. The following note or notes are fingered while blowing steadily.

There is a tendency to shorten the second note of the slur. Be sure to hold the second note for its full length, so that there is no pause between the slurs.

Here we learn a second fingering for E, indicated by EII. You have learned EI in the first lesson. The second fingering makes certain combinations of fingerings easier, and helps you to play fast passages, slurs, and trills more smoothly.

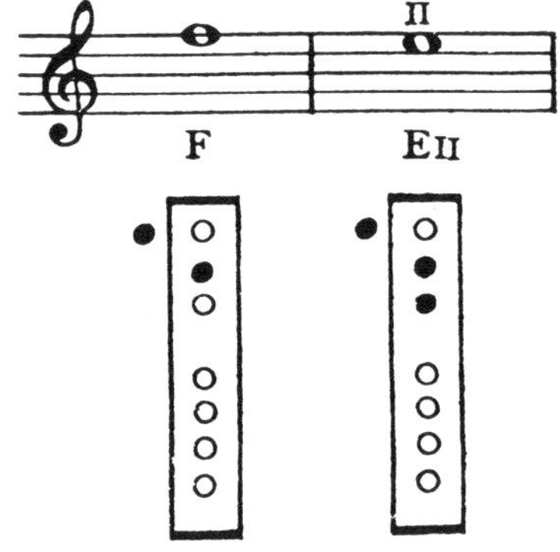

Try these combinations to see for yourself:

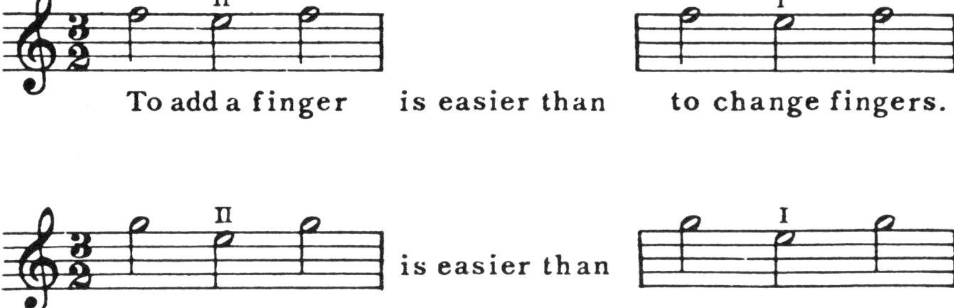

The rest of this lesson will be practise in playing EII. In the next lesson, you will learn how to decide which fingering is better.

To change from G to EII the second finger acts as an anchor, while the thumb and third finger move up and down exactly together.

Practise this exercise first without slurring:

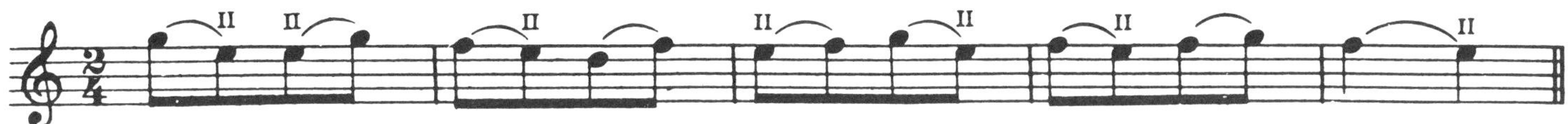

Slurring is a good way to check on your fingers. If you get an extra note, it is because your fingers don't find the holes right away, or are not released fast enough, or because your tongue is not synchronized with your fingers. Keep trying until it is fun.

SILENT, SILENT

German Folk Song

Is the second note of the slur as long as the first one?

LESSON III

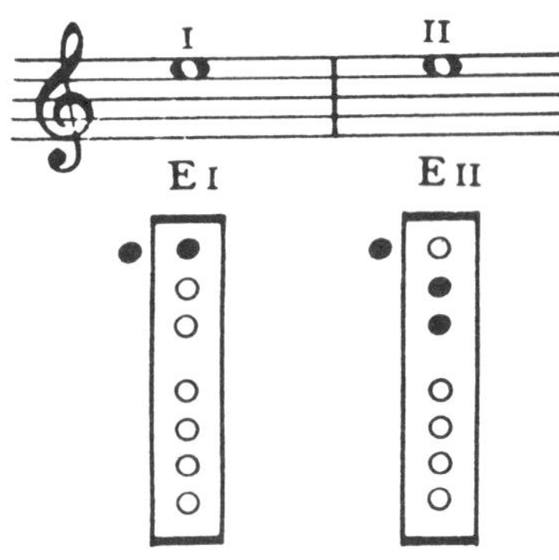

E

EI is fuller in tone and usually better in pitch than EII. It is, therefore, preferred on sustained notes.

EII is very practical for the fingering combinations mentioned in Lesson II, and for slurs and trills.

Learn to know both fingerings equally well.

Here you will find some suggestions for deciding which fingering to use.

In general, you will find it simpler to use EI when going *up* the scale, and EII when coming *down*.

Here is an exception where it is easier to slur by using the other fingering:

Learn this phrase by heart, with these fingerings:

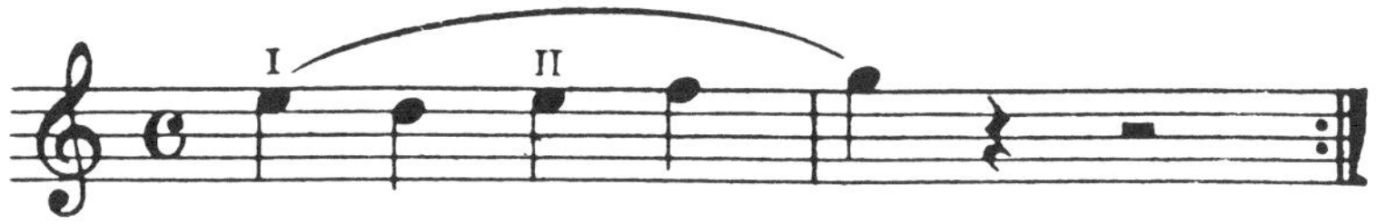

From: LA VOLTA

Play the slurs only when you are absolutely sure of your fingering.

THE PEASANT AND THE BEAR

TAMBOUR

DANCE MELODY FROM SILESIA

While playing with your friend, watch your tone very carefully. In a duet a singing tone is more important than a loud tone.

SIXTEENTH CENTURY GERMAN FOLK SONG

OLD GERMAN LULLABY

Now you should be able to decide for yourself when to play EI and when to play EII. Try the teacher's part in "Silent, Silent" in Lesson II. After you have decided which fingerings to use, play the duet with a friend.

* See page 7 for an explanation of $\frac{6}{8}$ time signature.

LESSON IV

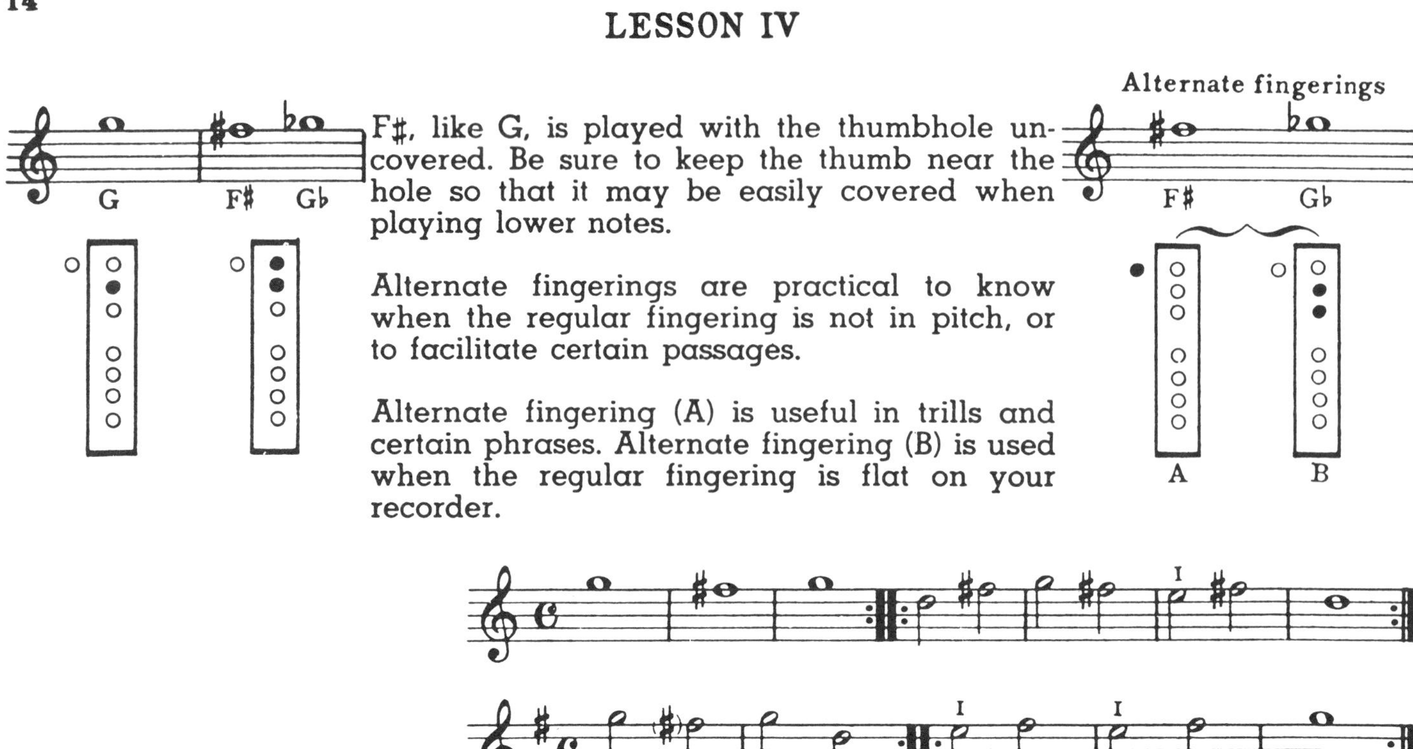

F♯, like G, is played with the thumbhole uncovered. Be sure to keep the thumb near the hole so that it may be easily covered when playing lower notes.

Alternate fingerings are practical to know when the regular fingering is not in pitch, or to facilitate certain passages.

Alternate fingering (A) is useful in trills and certain phrases. Alternate fingering (B) is used when the regular fingering is flat on your recorder.

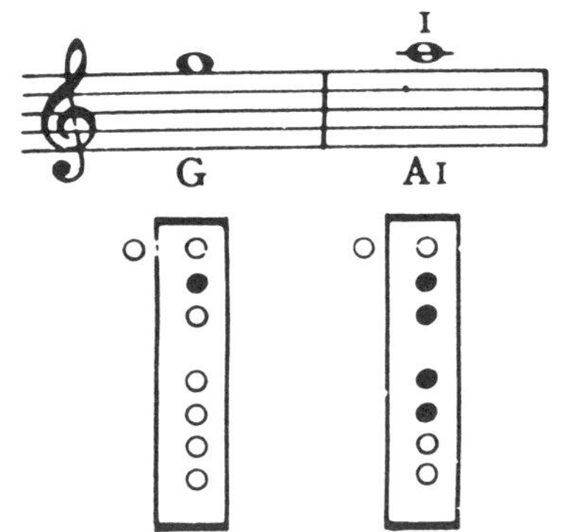

There are two fingerings for A, just as there were two for E. In this Lesson, we learn AI. It is learned first because it belongs to the first octave, and is played with the open thumbhole like F♯ and G.

Staccato:

A dot placed above or below a note shortens the length of the note to approximately half of its original value. Here "DuD̸" is pronounced crisply, as in the word "dot".

equals ‖ equals

Legato:

A dash above or below a note tells you to hold the note for its full value, which brings the neighboring notes very close together. A continuous flow of breath with a soft and fast "Du" to produce the new note will achieve the right legato effect.

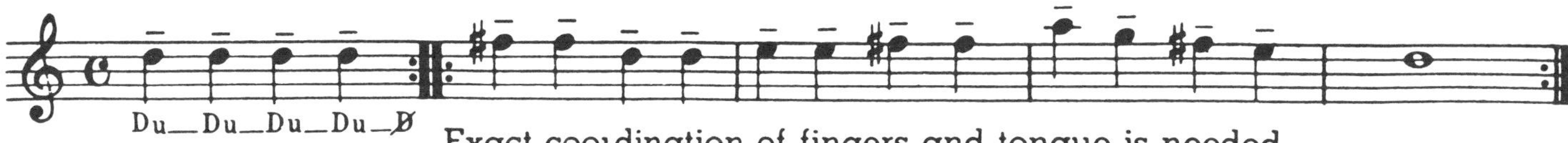

Exact coordination of fingers and tongue is needed.

Sharps or flats may be placed at the beginning of the line instead of directly in front of each note. They affect every note which is placed on the same line.

The contrast between staccato and legato must be used to give recorder music interest and variation, since there is no great possibility for dynamics without influencing the pitch.

A

In recorder music, you will find legato seldom indicated. Most of the time it is left to the player's interpretation. In this Lesson, it is indicated so that you may learn when to play legato. Later, you can apply it whenever you feel that the music asks for it.

Watch your 1/8 notes. Are they equally long?

A slur connecting two identical notes melts them together and is called a tie.

LESSON V

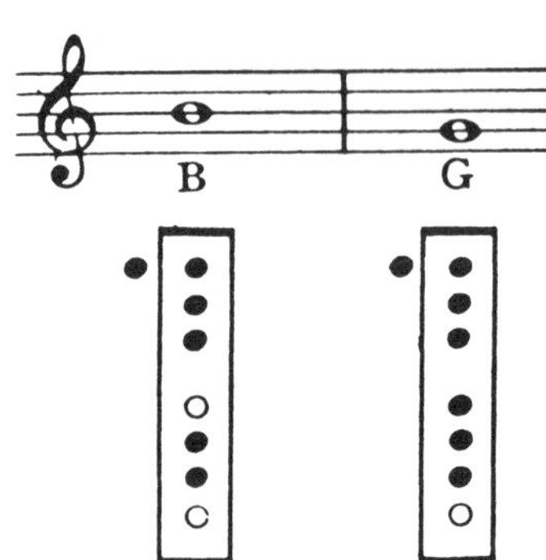

From now on you will be using the right hand. Be careful to keep both hands in position with the fingers directly above their holes so that they are ready to close them. Be sure that each hole is completely covered, for if any air leaks out you will get a squeak. Since the lower notes need less air, you should blow very carefully.

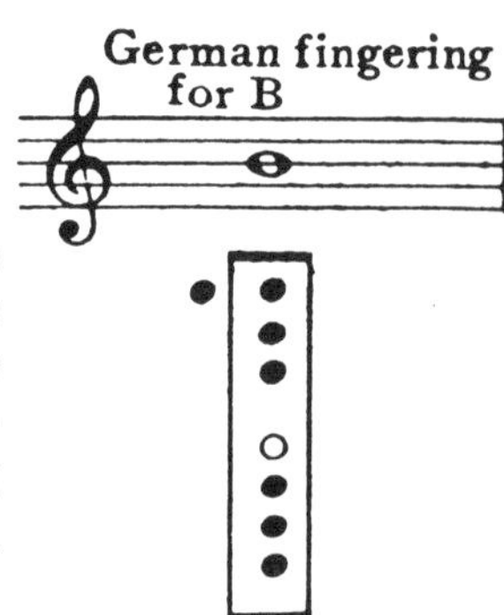

Use these whole-note exercises to practise breath control as described on page 5.

A Canon, or "Round" is a melody which harmonizes with itself. The first player begins at measure (1) and when he reaches measure (2) the second player begins at (1) while the first player continues. Most canons may be repeated as many times as desired. The ending can be done in two ways: Either the different parts stop one after the other at the end of the melody, or close together with a chord at the fermata. We have written out this first canon to show you how it should be played. Use the same rules for a canon with more than two parts.

DER WINTER IST VERGANGEN
German Folk Song
Pupil
A
Teacher
(Tenor Recorder)
II
I
SONG OF THE THREE HOLY KINGS
Austrian
Pupil
A
Teacher
A
IL ETAIT UN PETIT NAVIRE
French-Canadian Folk Song
Pupil
A
Teacher
A

LESSON VI

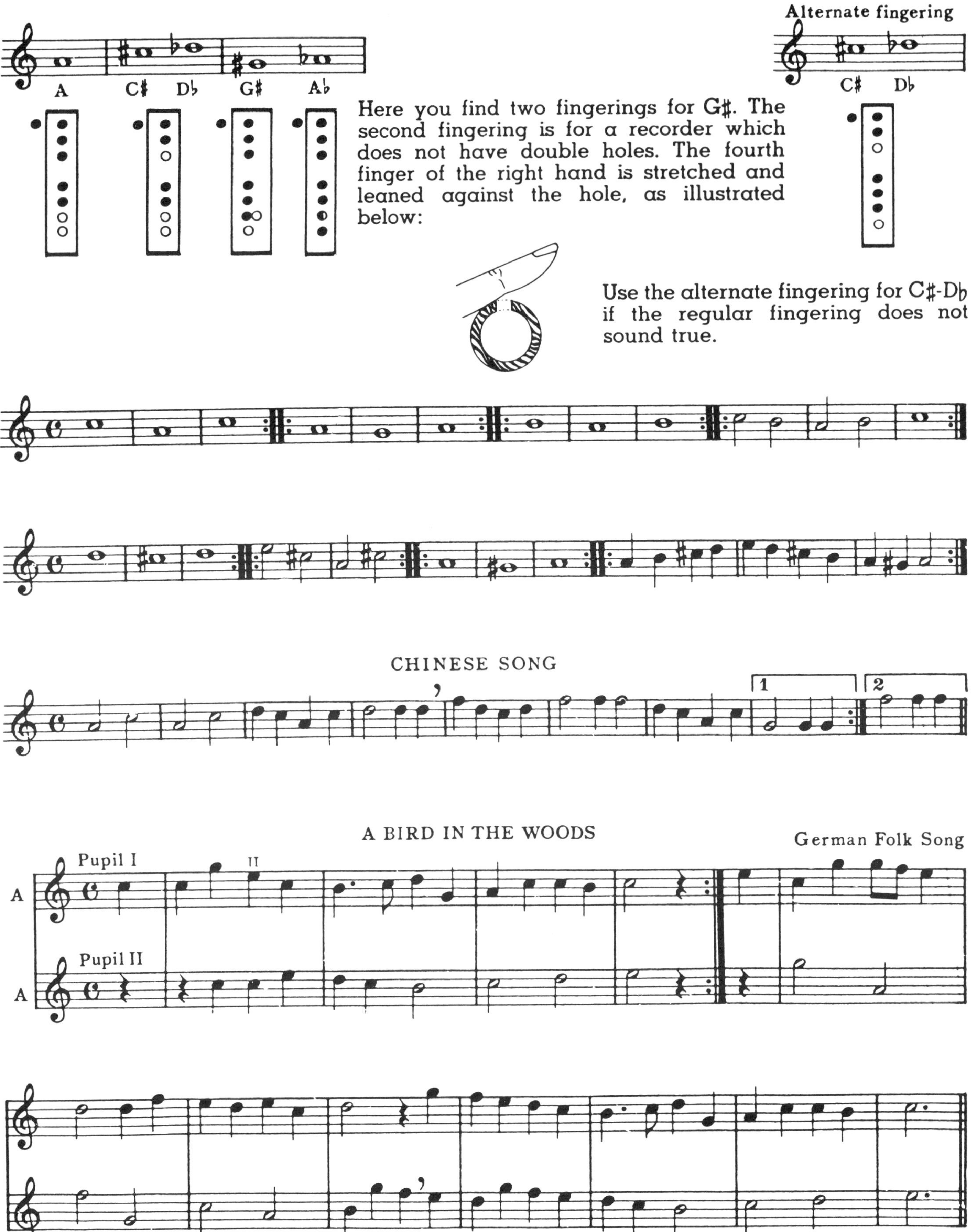
Alternate fingering
A
C♯
D♭
G♯
A♭
C♯
D♭
Here you find two fingerings for G♯. The second fingering is for a recorder which does not have double holes. The fourth finger of the right hand is stretched and leaned against the hole, as illustrated below:
Use the alternate fingering for C♯-D♭ if the regular fingering does not sound true.
CHINESE SONG
1
2
A BIRD IN THE WOODS
German Folk Song
Pupil I
A
II
Pupil II
A

This is a beautiful melody. Play it and phrase it so that it sings!

Next you come to the first Review Lesson. You can use everything you have learned in thes first six Lessons when you play it. Study it, and then return to it later and do it again, not only t review, but to enjoy the music!

REVIEW LESSON I

THE CUCKOO
German Folk Song
Pupil I
Pupil II
A
A
THE IRISH WASHERWOMAN
MARCH
Chédeville
Pupil I
Pupil II
FIVE PART CANON
Praetorius
1
2
3
4
5

LESSON VII

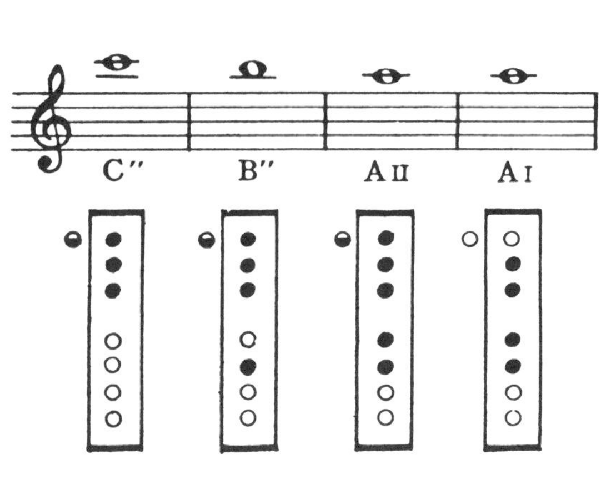

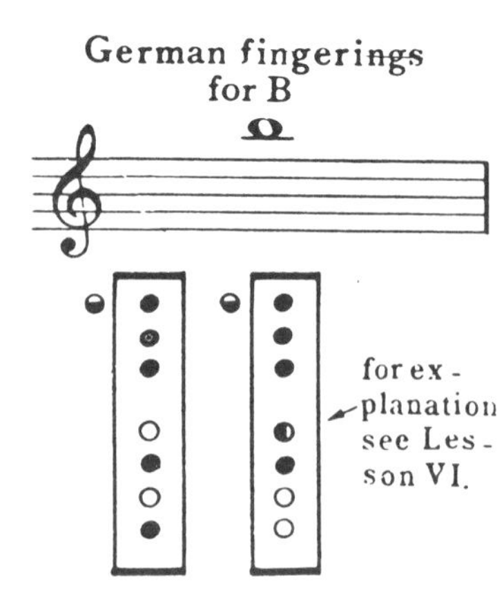

For the notes in the second, or higher octave starting with AII, you tip your thumb into the thumbhole so that the thumbnail goes *into* the hole, leaving a small opening at the top of the hole. The higher the note, the smaller this opening should be. If your nail is too long, the tip of your thumb will not close the lower part of the hole tightly, and the leaking air will cause a squeak.

C and AII have the same fingering as low C and A, except for the thumb position.

When changing to or from G, AI is usually easier. For most other combinations use AII, especially in connection with notes in the upper octave. Where the thumb is already in the octave position.

When you go from G to A and then to the upper octave, the change will be smoother if you use AI and then close the thumb and first finger for AII. Practise this exercise slowly until it becomes easy, and can be done smoothly and quickly.

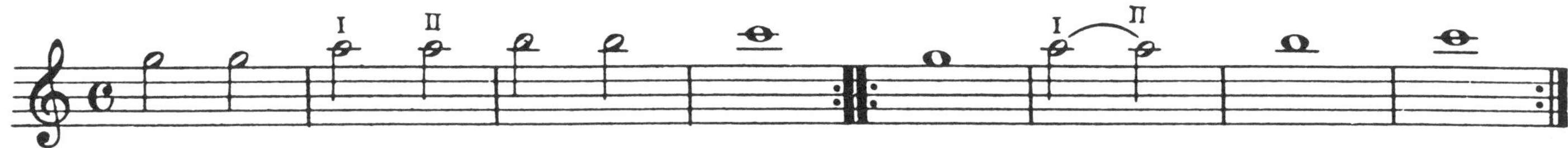

LITTLE BELLS OF WESTMINSTER

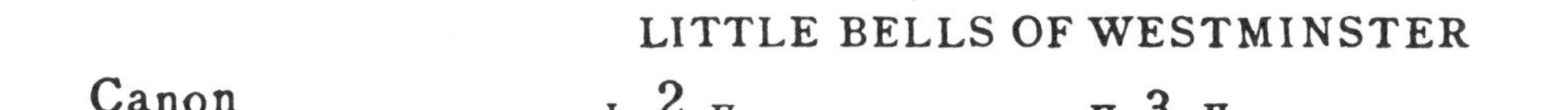

C'EST PAS LA BAGNE

VOM HIMMEL HOCH
J. S. Bach
JOY TO THE WORLD
Handel
Pupil I
Pupil II
A
A
DANCE
Melchior Frank
Pupil
Teacher
A
A

LESSON VIII

F F♯ G♭ B♭ A♯ B♭ A♯

on single hole recorder

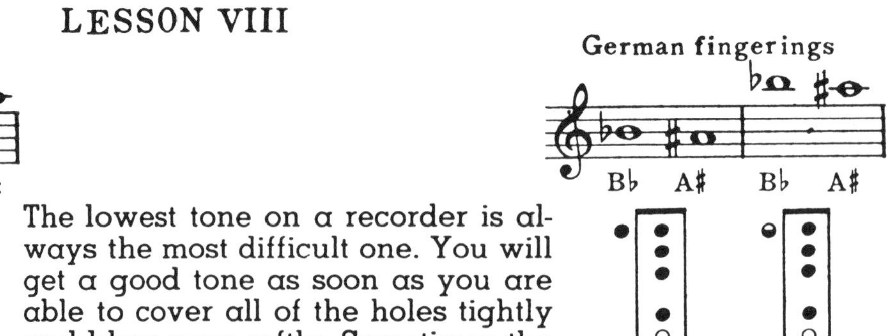

The lowest tone on a recorder is always the most difficult one. You will get a good tone as soon as you are able to cover all of the holes tightly and blow very softly. Sometimes the fingers of the left hand open up and cause a squeak. Don't give up. You will master it!

Remember to use these exercises for breath control also:

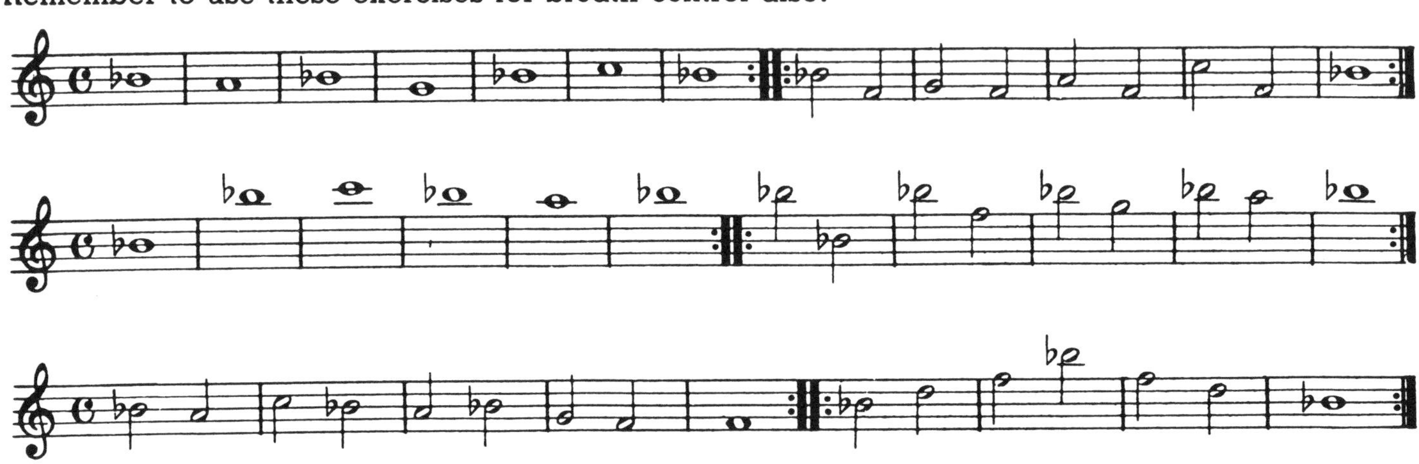

A LA CLAIRE FONTAINE

French-Canadian Folk Song

Be sure to play the second part, too, for it is good practise for the low F♯ and G♯.

PRAISE FOR BREAD

The more time you take for difficult fingerings or passages, the faster your progress will be.

Excerpt from SONATA II
Mattheson
Pupil I
Pupil II
A
A
I
II
WAYFARING STRANGER
American Folk Song
RIGADOON
Purcell
Pupil I
Pupil II
From BRANDENBURG CONCERTO No. 2
Allegro
J. S. Bach

LESSON IX

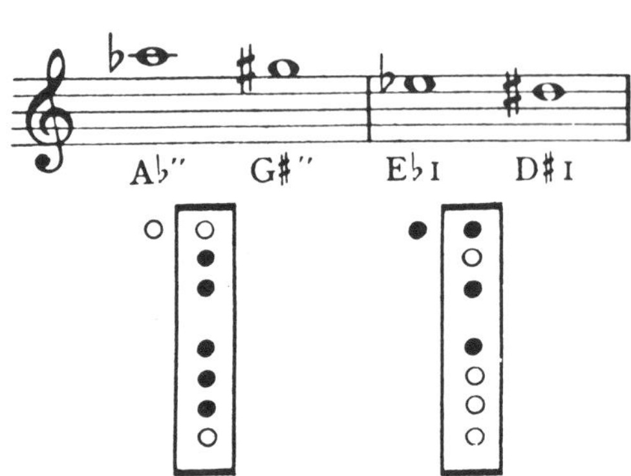

This Lesson is important, for E♭ and A♭ appear frequently in recorder music. Don't be tempted to ignore it. The high A♭ is easy to remember, for it is like AI with one more finger.

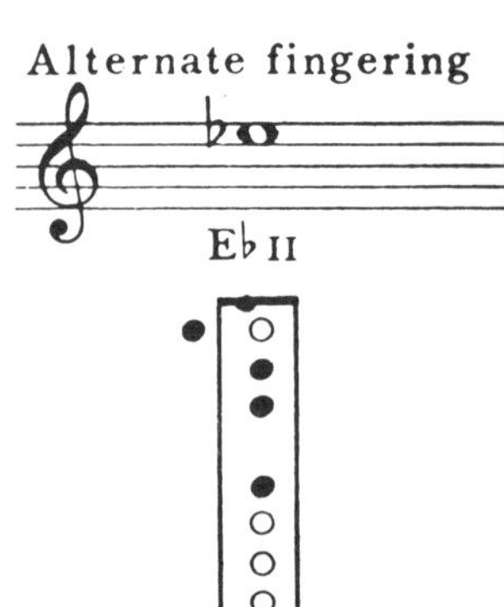

You have used these exercises for breath control. Don't you notice an improvement in your tone?

IHR KINDERLEIN KOMMET

German Christmas Carol
Melody by Johann Schulz (1747-1800)

C'ÉTAIT ANNE DE BRETAGNE

French-Canadian Folk Song

If you can master these four sharps and play this carol smoothly, you can be proud of yourself.

LESSON X

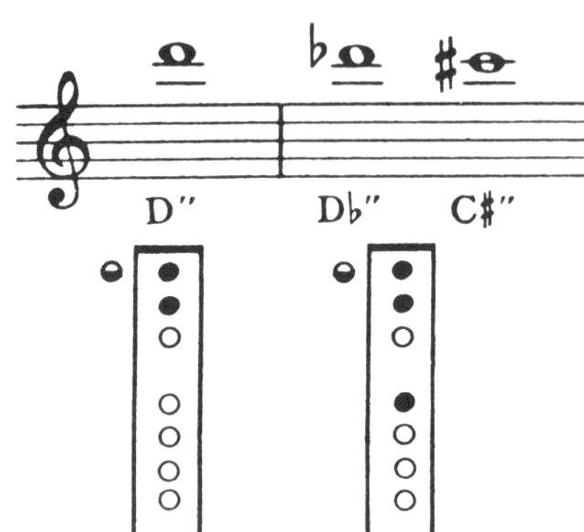

Remember that the higher the notes, the smaller the opening of the thumbhole should be. Press the thumbnail into the hole very firmly. Use enough breath to produce a clear tone. All notes above C require more air pressure.

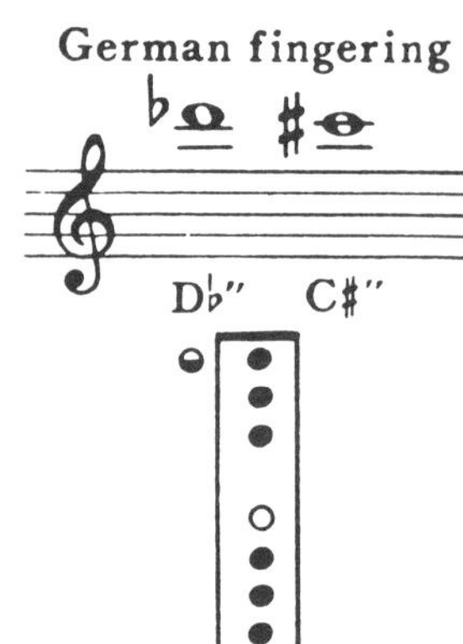

Every recorder has to be broken in gradually on the high notes starting with D. High-note exercises should not be played more than 20 minutes at a time for about the first six practise periods.

RETRAITE

English

KOMM SPIELMANN

Austrian Folk Dance

C'EST LA NUIT

French Folk Song

WEAVER'S DANCE

Austrian Folk Dance

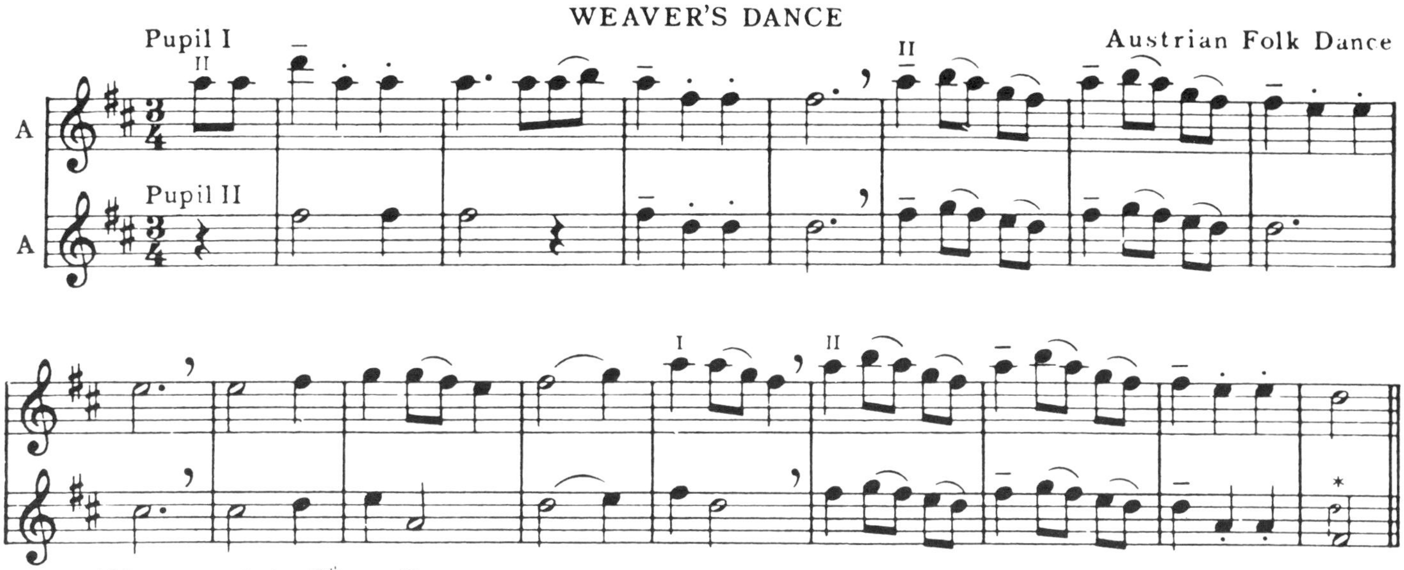
Pupil I
A
Pupil II
A

* If you cannot play F♯, use D.

GAVOTTE

G. F. Handel

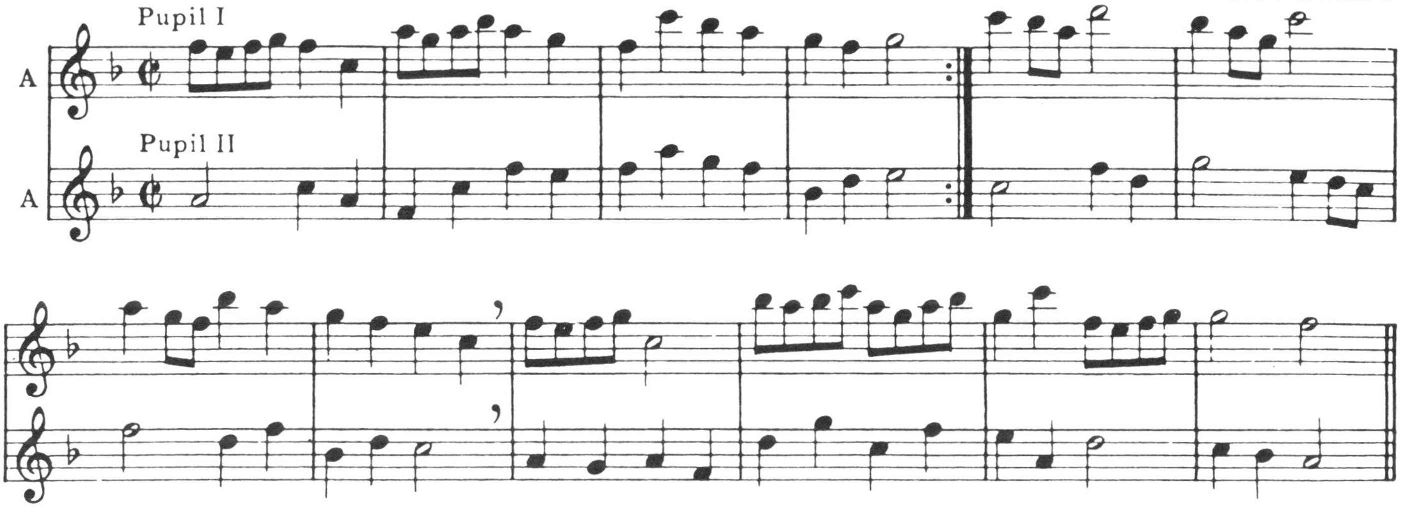
Pupil I
A
Pupil II
A

Here are two exercises for the ambitious student. They are taken from recorder solos by great masters, whom you will enjoy in your later explorations:

ALLEGRO from CAPRICCIO

G. F. Telemann

Excerpt from GIGA, SONATA in B♭ Major

Loeillet

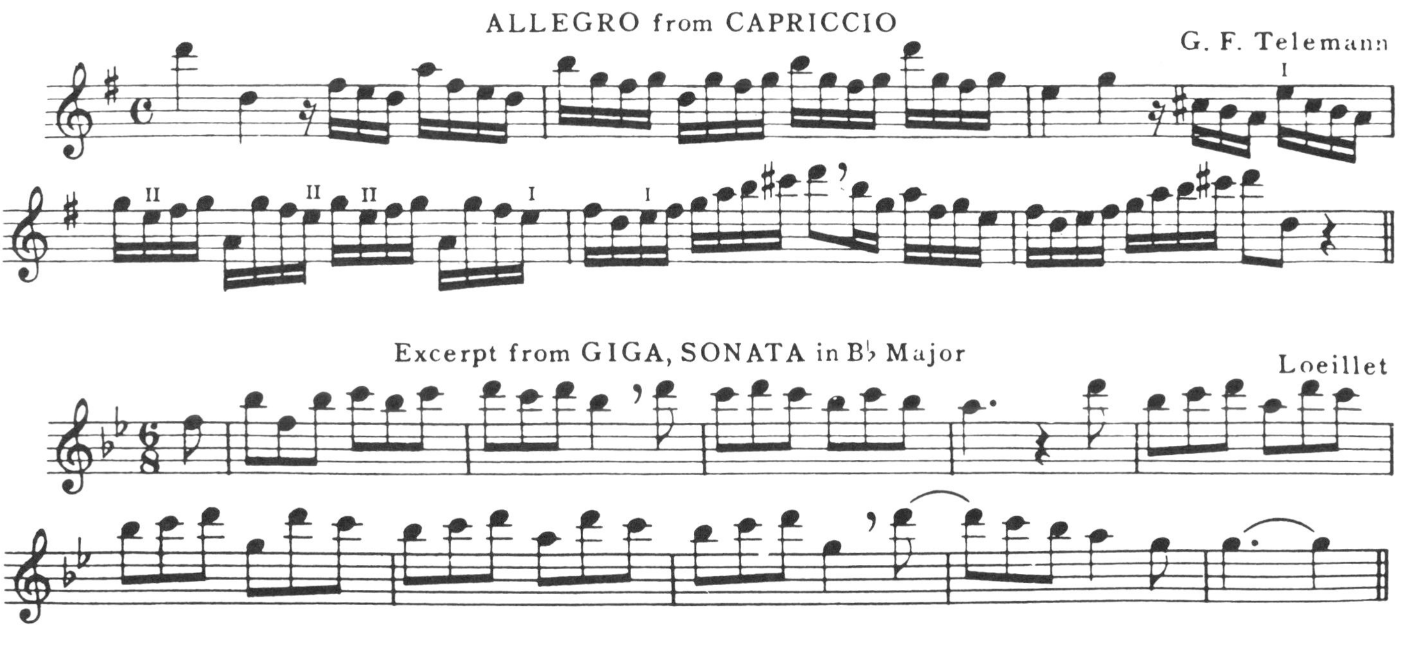

LESSON XI

This Lesson contains excerpts from three recorder sonatas which illustrate the high register as you will find it in original recorder music. After you master the high notes, try for expression.

A

* See Trill Chart

LESSON XII

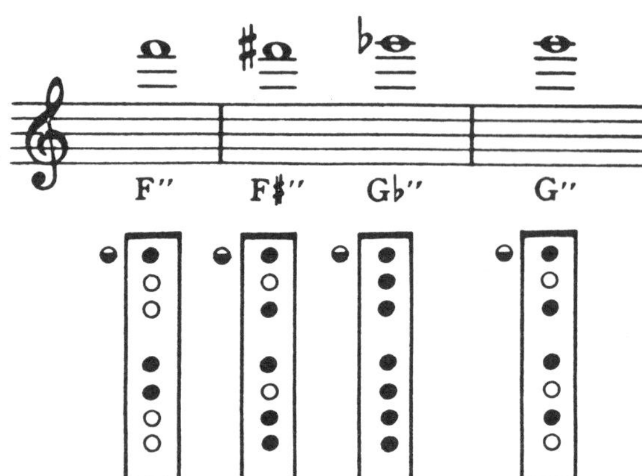

Now, in this last Lesson, you learn the highest notes. Practise them carefully and well. Remember to keep the thumbhole opening *very* small, and to blow harder than usual.

When you have finished this Lesson, go on to the Second Review on the next pages, and the Exercises. Then you are ready to explore recorder literature. You will find that you can play the music of the old masters easily, and there is much music available to suit the taste of every recorder player.

Enjoy Your Recorder!

You should learn this exercise by heart and use it to warm up the high register:

Now we have taught you all of the notes on the recorder. Play the chromatic scale up and down, to see if you remember the fingerings for all of the sharps and flats. Good luck!

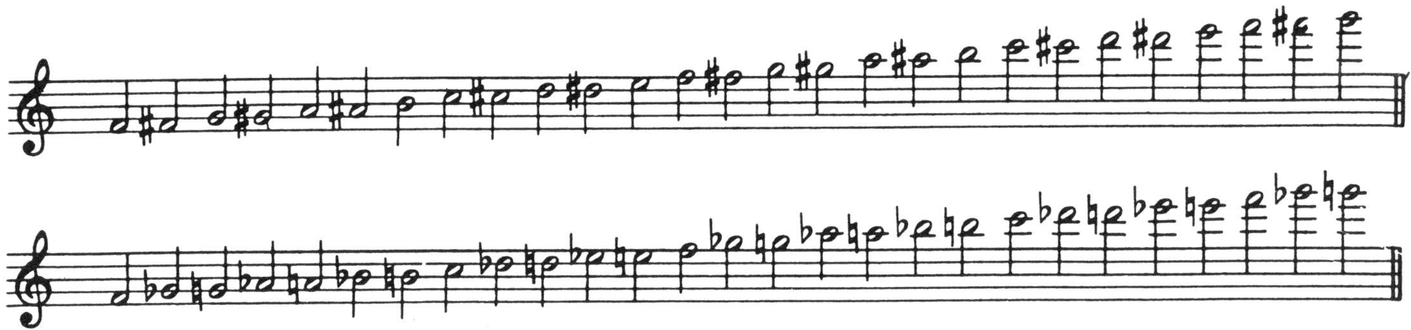

* See preceding exercise.

** See Lesson IX for explanation of E♭II.

REVIEW LESSON II

Arranged by Charlene Peterson
KERRY DANCERS
Irish
A
A
Fine
Faster
D.C. al Fine
From SONATA in CANON FORM
Telemann
A
A
1
2
Fine
D.C. al Fine
LIGHT OUR CANDLES
French-Canadian
A
A

Actual Ranges of the Recorder Family

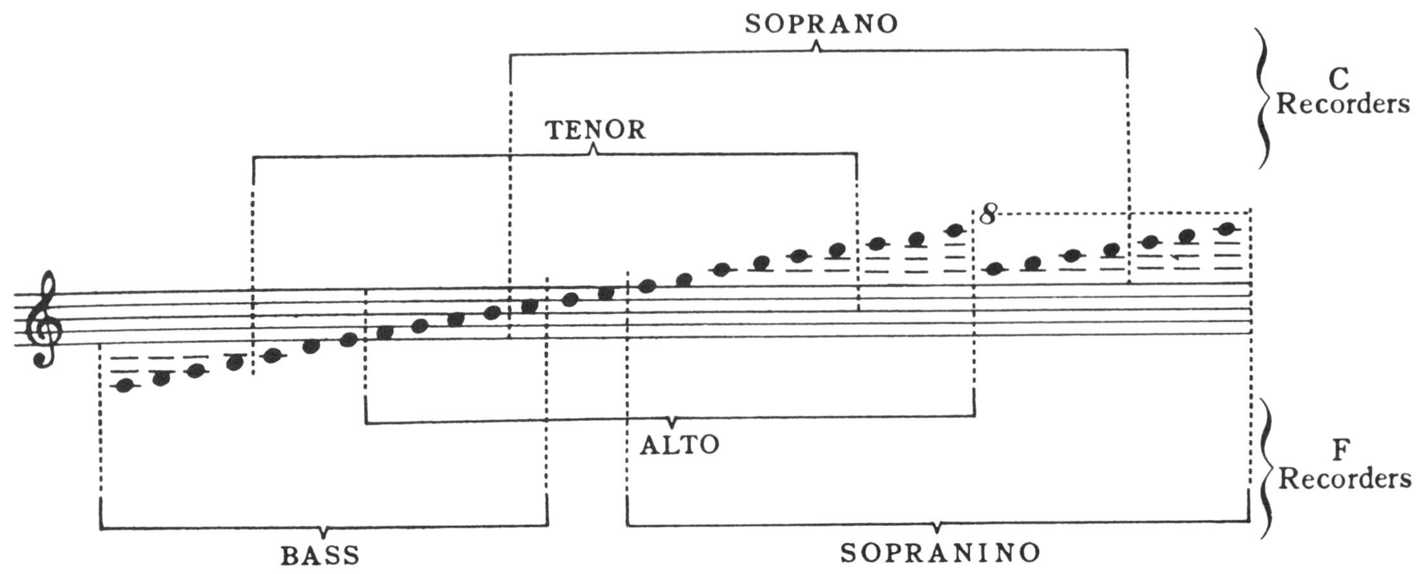

Written Ranges of the Recorder Family

Sopranino, Soprano, Bass } Sounds one octave higher than written

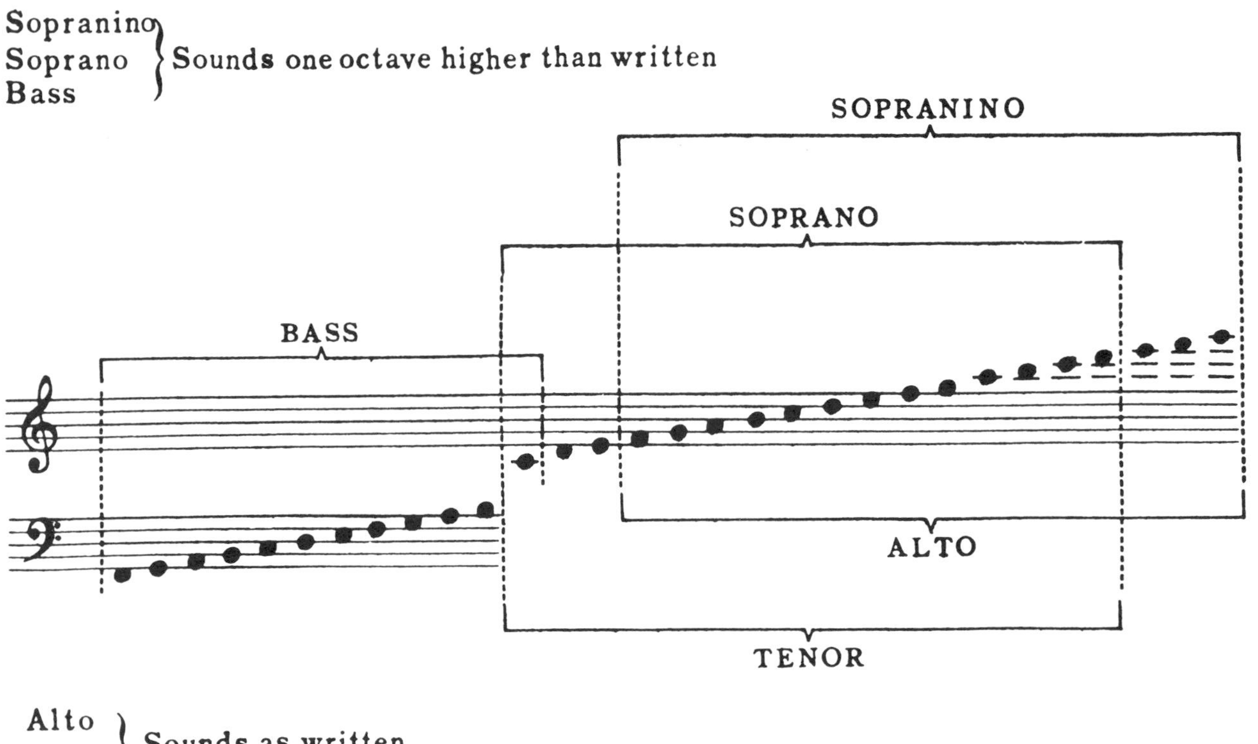

Alto, Tenor } Sounds as written

TRANSPOSITION FOR THE ALTO RECORDER

An Alto recorder player should be able to transpose an octave up, since some soprano parts are playable on an Alto recorder as long as it is within its range. Also, some recorder music is printed an octave lower than it sounds when played.

Example: Written for Soprano Recorder

If you want to play this melody, which is written for Soprano recorder, on the Alto recorder, you may transpose it to the proper range like this:

THE BASS RECORDER

The Bass recorder is not a solo instrument, but is very valuable in ensemble playing. If you play the Alto recorder and know the Bass clef, you will find it easy to play the Bass recorder, which is also an F instrument, just an octave lower.

This Canon is given just to show you that the Alto and Bass recorders have the same fingering:

CANON
(for Alto and Bass Reorders)

Sartorius

THE SOPRANINO RECORDER

The Sopranino recorder is also fingered exactly like the Alto recorder, but is just an octave higher.

A Sopranino can take the place of a Piccolo, as in "Change of the Guards" at the Danish Palace.

Handel uses it in the opera "Rinaldo" together with two Alto recorders and a soprano voice.

It will show its brilliance in imitating bird songs; Couperin's "Rossignol en Amour" and "The Bird Fancier's Delight" compiled by Dorothy C. Dana.

"CHANGE OF GUARDS" at the Danish Royal Palace
(for Sopranino Recorder)

EXERCISES
To Achieve Greater Facility

Most of these exercises are phrases or excerpts from Sonatas by Old Masters, as you will find them in Recorder Literature.

Five suggestions for practising Exercise **1** in different combinations of slurred, staccato and legato notes.

Eight suggestions for practising Exercises **2**, **3** and **5** in different combinations of slurred, staccato and legato notes.

*simile indicates that the phrasing marked in the first measure continues for all similar measures.

Phrases from Sonatas by Telemann

From a Sonata by Handel
13
GIGUE
14
Telemann
A
15
B
From a Sonata by Telemann
A
16
B
From a Sonata by Telemann
17

FINGERING CHART FOR TRILLS

B: Baroque Fingered Recorder only.
G: German Fingered Recorder only.

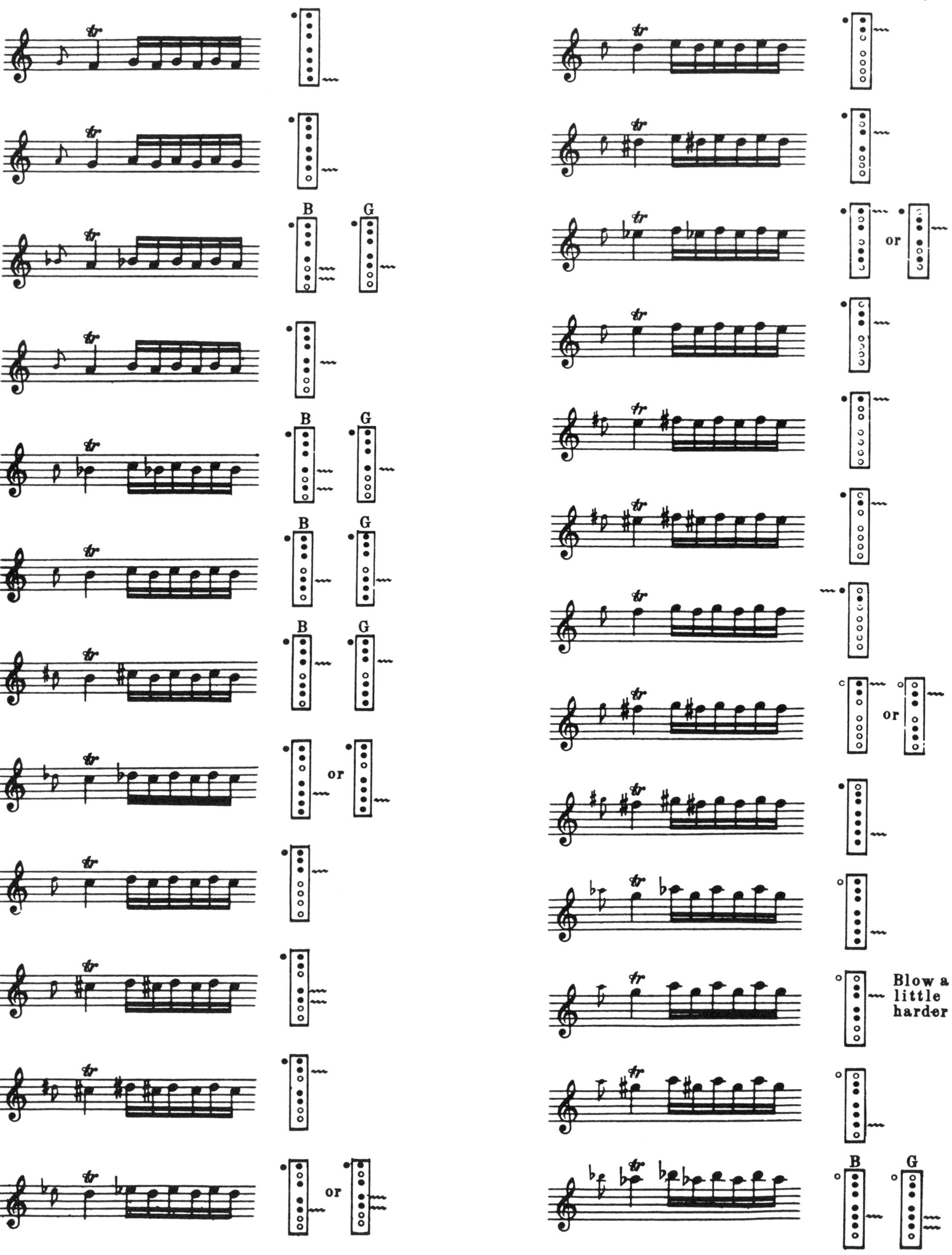

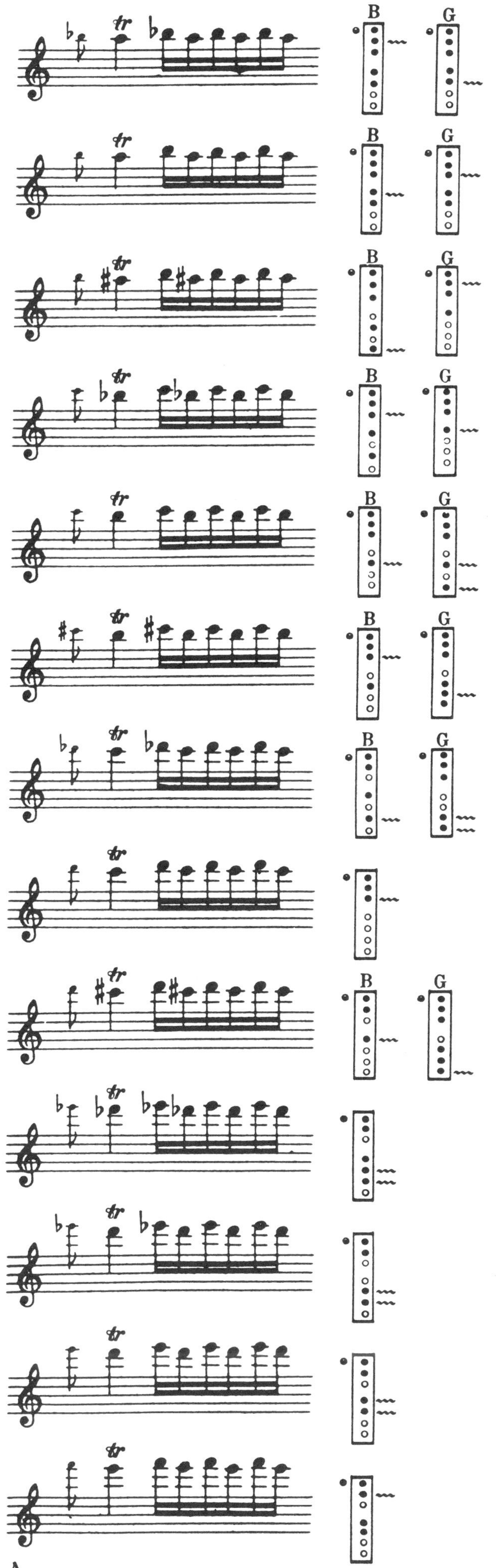

A

SOME ORNAMENTS OR EMBELLISHMENTS AND HOW TO PLAY THEM

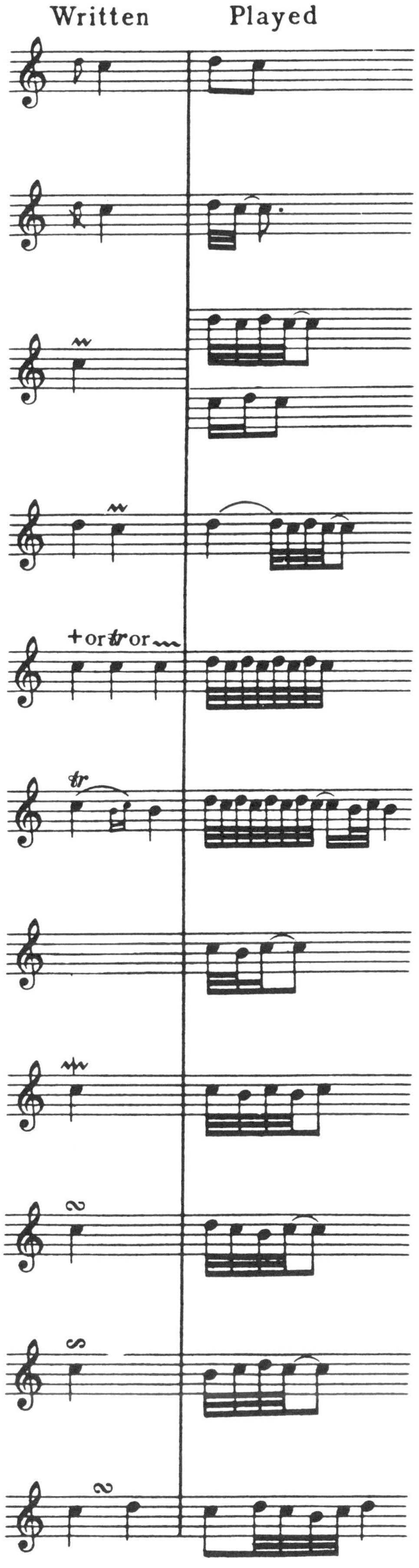

Written Played

Appoggiatura

Short Appoggiatura

Inverted Mordent Old Interpretation

Modern Interpretation

Inverted Mordent preceded by the same upper note

+ or tr or

Trill

Mordent

Extended Mordent

Turn

Turn placed between notes

PASSEPIED
K. Fischer
1
2
Sop.
Alto
OZARK MOUNTAIN FOLK TUNE
Sop.
Alto
AUSTRIAN YODEL
Slowly
Sop.
Alto

MARCH
Austria
Sop.
Alto
IT WAS CANDLEMAS DAY
Sop.
Alto
ZEPPERL POLKA
Austrian Folk Dance
Sop.
Alto
Fine
D.C. al Fine

LES CISEAUX DE LA VIERGE

* Alto play an octave higher.

SARABANDE
Johann Pezel 1675
Alto
Alto or Tenor
Bass
BALLO
Johann Pezel 1675
Alto
Alto or Tenor
Bass

LOBT GOTT IHR CHRISTEN

J.S. Bach

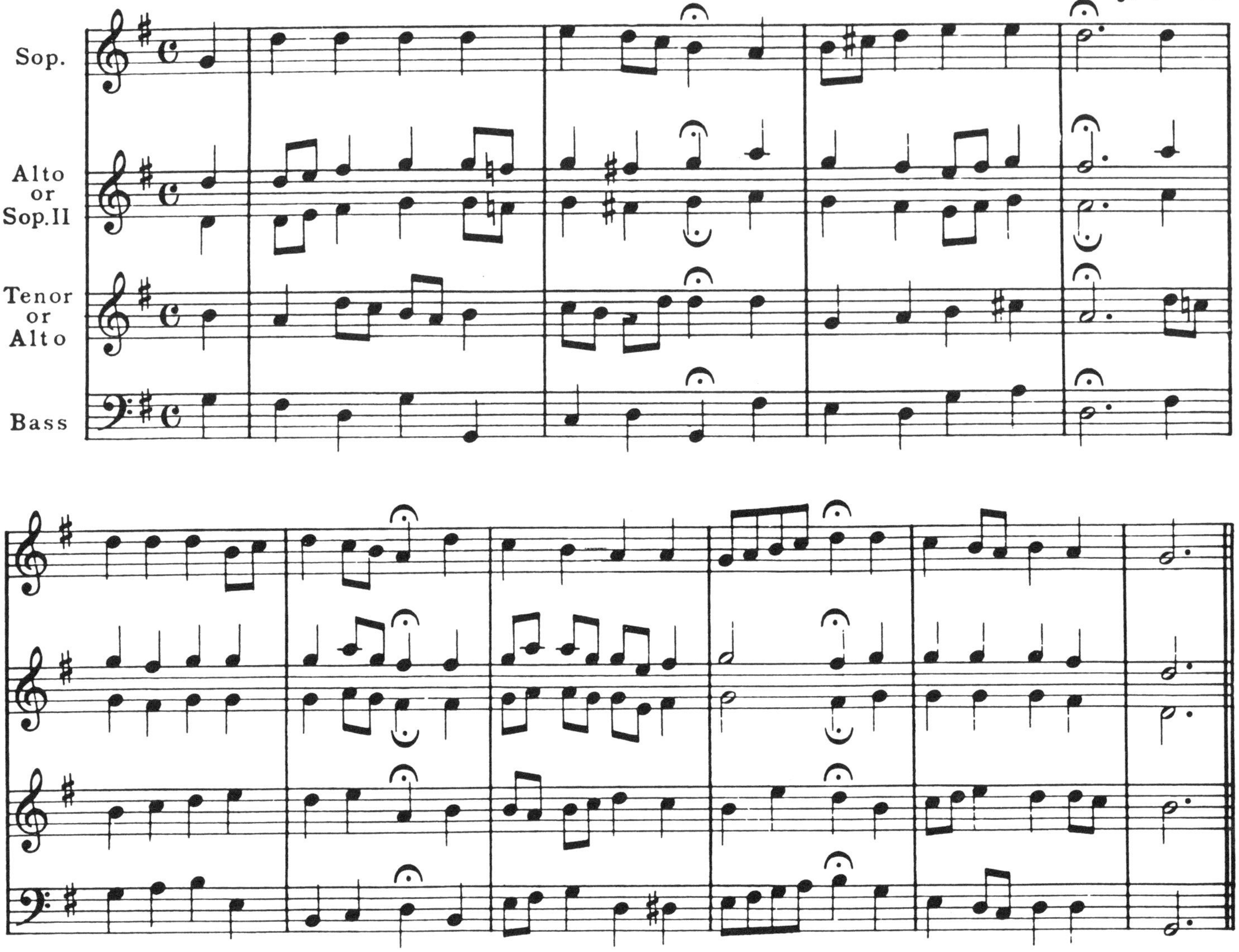
Sop.
Alto or Sop. II
Tenor or Alto
Bass

MEERSTERN ICH DICH GRÜSSE

German Pilgrimage Song

1
2
Sop.
Alto or Sop. II
Tenor or Alto
Bass
or
Tenor

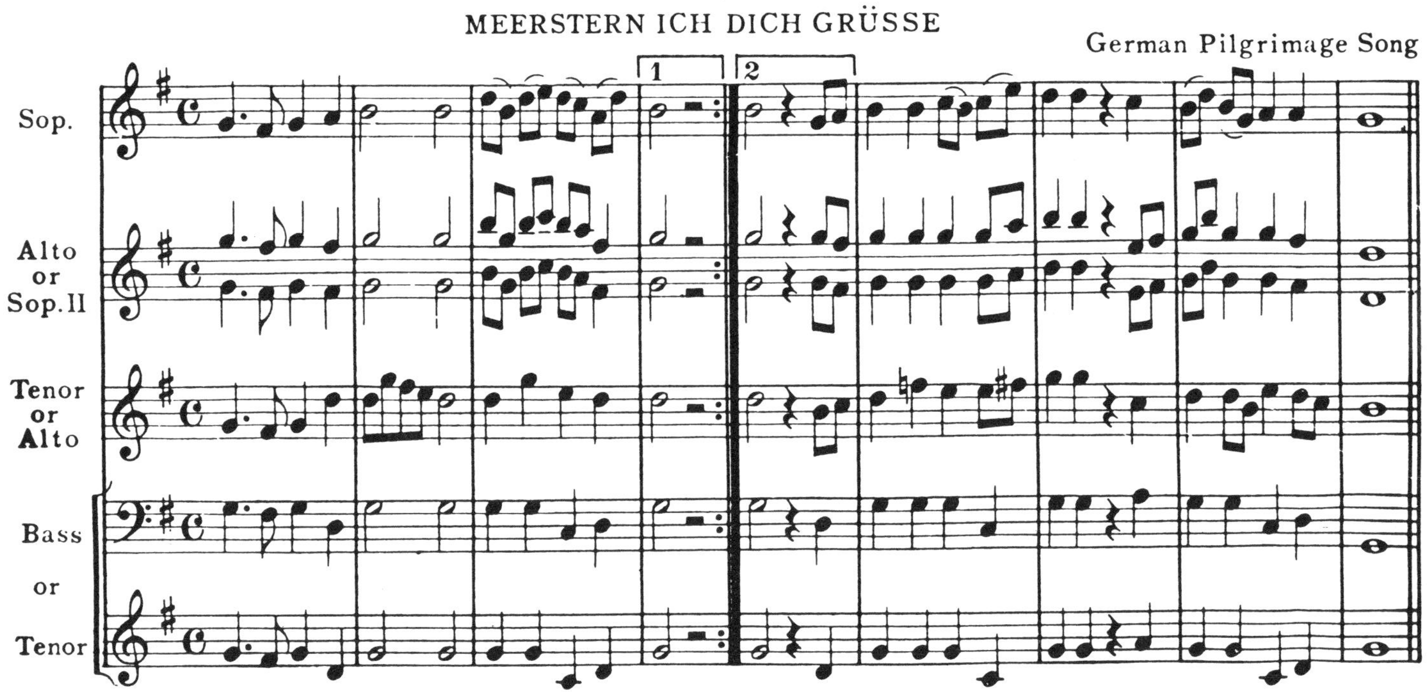